Photosynthesis

Torrey Maloof

Consultant

Leanne Iacuone, M.A.T., NBCT, ATC
Riverside Unified School District

Image Credits: p.27 Blend Images/Alamy;
pp.20–21 (bottom) Cultura Creative/Alamy;
pp.12–13 (illstrations) Tim Bradley; pp.8–9
(background) Lonely Planet Images/Getty Images;
pp.8–9 Inhabitos; pp.2–4, 6–7, 10–11 (bottom),
12–14, 15 (bottom) 19, 22–25 (background), 25–26,
30–32 iStock; p.17 (top) Nossant Jean Michel/
SIPA/Newscom; p.21 (top) Reuters/Newscom; p.5
NOAA; p.20 (left) NOAA MESA Project; p.15 (top &
middle) Diego Stocco/Gianfilippo De Rossi; p.11
(top) Fletcher & Baylis/Science Source; pp.28–29
(illustrations) Janelle Bell-Martin; all other images
from Shutterstock.

Library of Congress Cataloging-in-Publication Data

Maloof, Torrey, author.
  Photosynthesis / Torrey Maloof.
    pages cm
  Summary: "Have you ever seen a tree at the grocery
store buying dinner? Probably not! Plants create their
food in a very different way. They make their own food
through photosynthesis"—Provided by publisher.
  Audience: K to grade 3.
  Includes index.
  ISBN 978-1-4807-4640-4 (pbk.)
  ISBN 1-4807-4640-1 (pbk.)
  ISBN 978-1-4807-5084-5 (ebook)
  1. Photosynthesis—Juvenile literature.
  2. Plants—Juvenile literature. I. Title.
  QK882.M285 2015
  572.46—dc23
                                    2014034231

Teacher Created Materials

5301 Oceanus Drive
Huntington Beach, CA 92649-1030
http://www.tcmpub.com
ISBN 978-1-4807-4640-4

Table of Contents

Solar Energy

All living things on Earth need **energy** to live. You need energy. Animals need energy. And plants need energy, too. Plants get energy from a star that we know as the sun.

The sun is a massive and mighty star. It sends light and heat in every direction. A small portion of its solar energy shines on Earth. Its sunlight packs a powerful punch. It heats our planet and creates wind. It supports the water cycle. It also supplies plants with the energy they need to grow.

The sun heats water. Water **evaporates** into the sky. It turns to **vapor**, **condenses**, and forms clouds. Then, it rains. The water collects in lakes, rivers, and streams. Then, it evaporates again, and the cycle continues. The water cycle provides the moisture plants and animals need to survive.

condensation

condensation

precipitation

precipitation

evaporation

evaporation

Humans are learning to use solar energy, too. Scientists are finding ways to use the sun's light to power cars, homes, and even our phones!

stem

leaves

roots

Bamboo is a fast-growing plant. Some types of bamboo can grow more than one meter (three feet) in one day!

6

Parts of a Plant

Plants can grow almost anywhere on Earth. They grow in the ocean. They grow in the mountains. They even grow in deserts! There arc 300,000 types of plants in our world. Plants have features that help them live in these places. But all plants rely on the same things to survive. They all need sun, water, air, and food. They also all have the same parts to help them live.

Mighty Moss

It might not look quite like other plants, but moss can do some incredible things. Could you survive under an arctic layer of ice for 1,500 years? An ancient piece of moss was able to do just that! When scientists pulled it out of the ice, they gave it a little light and warmth. Soon, it was good as new—and growing again!

Growing Bridges

Roots aren't just for plants anymore. The War-Khasis tribe of India creates bridges from the roots of rubber trees! It takes 10 to 15 years for a bridge to grow. These bridges are strong enough to support the weight of 50 people!

Roots

Have you ever thought about why plants don't blow away when it's windy? Or why they don't wash away when it's raining? It's because plants have strong and sturdy roots. Roots anchor plants into the ground. They grow underneath the soil. Humans absorb the **nutrients** they need to live and grow from food. But plants use their roots to absorb nutrients from the soil.

Root Recipes

Roots can be the tastiest part of a plant. We eat the roots of carrots, turnips, rutabagas, potatoes, and onions.

red onions

Roots don't just hold plants into the ground. They also hold soil in place and help keep Earth healthy.

Different plants have different roots. Some plants have a **taproot** system. This means they have one big root from which little roots grow. This type of root can grow very long. It lets the plant get water from deep under the soil. Large trees have a taproot system. Other plants have a fibrous root system in which a bunch of thin roots grow from the stem of the plant. These roots stay shallow. Garden plants usually have a fibrous root system.

Not all roots grow underground. Some rise from the stem. They hang in the air or stretch through the air before working their way underground. Corn has this type of root system.

Scientists found a tree in Sweden with roots that have been growing for more than 9,500 years!

fibrous root system

Scientists are studying how plants use roots and soil to warn one another about diseases.

taproot system

Plant Food

When plants and animals die, they **decompose**. This means they dissolve, or break apart. As they decompose, they are absorbed into the soil. This is what makes dirt rich with nutrients and the perfect meal for new plants.

Stems

Stems are strong. They have to be because they have an important job to do. Stems hold up and support the leaves and flowers of plants. They are the plant's backbone. As a plant gets older, the stem grows longer and thicker. The outside of the stem becomes rough so that it can protect the plant.

The inside of a stem acts as a road system for plants. Tiny tubes carry water and nutrients throughout the plant. Stems also store nutrients for plants to use later.

Snacking on Stems

Celery is a great after-school snack. It's also a fun way to study stems. When we eat celery, we eat the long, strong stem of the celery plant.

Water and minerals travel through the stem, up through the roots, to the rest of the plant.

Straight to the Top!

Just like a straw, stems carry water—and whatever else they find—to the top of the plant. Grab some simple supplies to get a closer look at how stems work.

Let the celery sit in the water overnight. What do you notice in the morning?

Have and adult cut the celery.

Fill jars with water.

Add food coloring.

Leaves

Have you ever gathered a big pile of leaves and then jumped into it? Have you made an art project with leaves? Leaves are beautiful. They are also an important part of every plant. There are many different types of leaves. Some are big and some are small. Some are smooth and glossy. Others are rough and have jagged edges. Some are green, and others may be brown or orange.

Leaves are where plants make their food. It happens in the part of the leaf called the *blade*. The food then moves through a leaf's **veins** to the stalk. The stalk is the part of a leaf that connects to the stem. All of these parts work together to help the plant grow big and strong.

blade

vein

stem

stalk

Rock On!

People are always coming up with new ways to use plants! Sound expert Diego Stocco (dee-EY-goh STO-koh) uses leaves to play a record! They work just like a needle on a record player! He turns and layers the leaves to produce different sounds.

Leaf Names

Leaves come in many shapes and sizes. Long, thin pine needles are leaves. The large leaves on a palm tree are called *fronds*.

Making Food

Have you ever seen a plant eating food? Probably not. That's because plants are some of the only living things that can make their own food. For many years, this process was a mystery. But today, we know how plants do it. The process is called **photosynthesis**. It's a simple, but amazing process. Water. Sunlight. Air. That's all it takes to make the energy that plants use to grow!

water + sunlight +

A Bright Idea

Plants are responsible for most of the photosynthesis that happens on Earth. But algae (AL-jee)—which aren't quite plants or animals—also use photosynthesis to make food. Scientist, Pierre Calleja (pee-AIR kai-YAY-ha), uses these creatures to create eco-friendly lamps. No electricity needed. These lamps are powered by the algae's photosynthesis!

air

growing, growing, growing!

sunlight energy

oxygen

carbon dioxide

glucose

water

Water is made up of two parts:

hydrogen (H_2) and one part oxygen (O).

That's why people call water H_2O.

18

Photosynthesis begins with the sun. Without the sun, plants would not have the energy needed to make food. **Chlorophyll** (KLAWR-uh-fil) in a plant's leaves absorbs light from the sun.

Water is also essential to plants because it is made up of **hydrogen** and **oxygen**. Plant roots absorb water from the ground. Then, the hydrogen in the water is used to create energy.

Plants also use **carbon dioxide** from the air. Chlorophyll changes the carbon dioxide and hydrogen. It transforms them into glucose, or sugar, that plants use for energy.

Fall Colors

Chlorophyll is what gives plants their color. In the fall, there is less sunlight. The days are shorter. Leaves absorb less sun, so they start making less chlorophyll. Soon, leaves stop making chlorophyll. This is why leaves change colors.

Bigger Effects

Photosynthesis gives plants energy. It also helps humans. Plants use the hydrogen in water and release oxygen into the air. If plants did not release this oxygen, we would not be able to breathe. We need oxygen to live! All animals breathe oxygen.

Plants also use carbon dioxide to make food. This is a good thing because too much carbon dioxide in the air isn't good for humans. It can actually become poisonous! Plants take carbon dioxide out of the air. This helps keep our air clean and healthy.

Phytoplankton are tiny organisms that live on the ocean's surface. They create more than half of the oxygen we need to breathe.

phytoplankton

Clearing the Air

Forests are rich in trees—and oxygen. But cities are often filled with pollution, and oxygen can be tough to find. So city planners are bringing forests into the city! Vertical farms and forests help city dwellers grow their own food and clean the air.

Photosynthesis produces energy. The same energy that plants use to survive also feeds other living things. Birds, insects, and mammals, including people, rely on plants for food. And we do more than eat plants. We also eat the animals that rely on these plants. The energy is passed to us through the animals we eat. In one way or another, we get all our energy from plants.

snake

hawk

rat

A Food Chain

grasshopper

plants

Talk to a Plant

Gardeners have long believed that talking to plants can help them grow! An online experiment is testing this theory with messages from people around the world. Visit **http://www.talktoaplant.com** to learn more.

Spoken to
➡ 45.7 cm (18 in.) tall
➡ darker green
➡ exposed to over 68,000 words

Silent
➡ 40.6 cm (16 in.) tall
➡ smaller leaves
➡ exposed to zero words

Plants have many other benefits, too. Many plants are famous for their ability to heal. Oranges can prevent colds. They contain vitamin C. Ginger can relieve upset stomachs. People put ginger in their beverages to soothe their tummies. Lavender can help people relax. Many lotions and bubble baths come in lavender scent to help people unwind.

Have you ever gotten a sunburn? It stings! Aloe (AL-oh) vera plants can help. There is a special gel in the leaves of these plants. The gel can help heal burns and small cuts.

Without photosynthesis, none of these plants would exist.

True Value of a Plant

In 1638, in Holland, a person traded 4 oxen, 8 pigs, 12 sheep, a bed, clothes, and 1,000 pounds of cheese for 1 tulip bulb!

Curing with Chlorophyll

Some people take chlorophyll pills to prevent bad breath. Others use it to help with digestion. Doctors are still studying how it works. Spinach, parsley, and green beans all have high levels of chlorophyll.

green beans

orange

ginger

aloe vera

lavender

The Power of Plants

Inhale. Exhale. Inhale. Exhale. We have plants to thank for every breath we take! If we didn't have plants, we wouldn't have oxygen. Without oxygen, we wouldn't be able to breathe. Plants also take carbon dioxide out of the air, making it healthier for us to breathe. If we didn't have plants, we wouldn't have food. Without food, we wouldn't have energy to live and grow.

Plants are a vital part of our world. They help us thrive in so many different ways. That's exactly why it's so important that we take care of them. Inhale. Exhale. Inhale. Exhale. Thank you, plants!

Making Music

Artist Ryuichi (ru-EE-chee) Sakamoto has found a way to translate photosynthesis activity into music. He calls his creation the Forest Symphony Project. You can listen to the sounds produced by 24 Japanese trees at **http://vimeo.com/82765073**.

Think Like a Scientist

What do plants need for photosynthesis?
Experiment and find out!

What to Get

- camera
- cardboard
- grass seed
- potting soil
- shallow aluminum pan
- water

What to Do

1. Place a layer of soil in the aluminum pan. Plant the seeds in the soil.

2. Water the soil. (**Note:** Be sure not to overwater the soil. Too much water will prevent the grass from growing.) Put the pan in a place that gets sun. Make sure the soil stays moist for one week.

3. Allow the grass to grow half an inch. Record the color of the grass with a photograph.

4. Cover a third of the pan with a piece of cardboard. (Remove it only to water.) Stop watering the middle third of grass. Water the other grass as normal.

5. After a week, remove the cardboard. Compare the grass color to the color of the grass in the photograph. Take photographs and use a table like the one below to record what happened. Discuss with a parent, a teacher, or a friend why this may have happened.

	Sun and Water	Sun only	Water only
Week 1			
Week 2			

Glossary

carbon dioxide—a gas that is produced when people and animals breathe out

chlorophyll—the green substance in plants that makes it possible for them to make food from carbon dioxide and water

condenses—changes from a gas into a liquid

decompose—to slowly break down

energy—power that can be used to do something

evaporates—changes from a liquid into a gas

hydrogen—the most common element that has no color or smell

nutrients—substances that living things need to live and grow

oxygen—a gas that is found in the air and is necessary for life

photosynthesis—the process in which plants use sunlight to combine water and carbon dioxide to make their own food (glucose)

taproot—the large main root of a plant from which smaller roots grow

vapor—a substance in the form of a gas

veins—thin lines that can be seen on the surface of a leaf

Index

Your Turn!

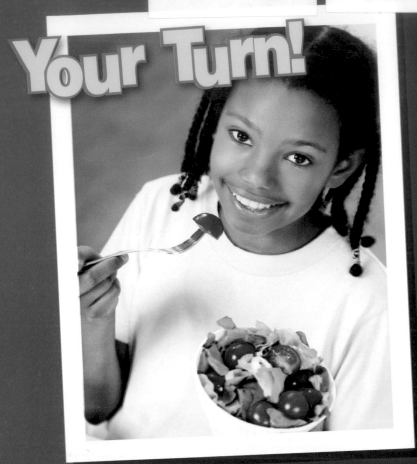

Yummy Plants

Plants help humans in lots of ways. They make oxygen for us to breathe. They take carbon dioxide out of the air. They anchor our soil to keep land in place. Plants also supply us with over 2,000 kinds of food.

Think about all the plants you eat. List as many as you can in five minutes. Then, grab an adult and make a yummy salad!